FAR VOYAGES

Books by Douglas LePan

FAR VOYAGES

poems

by

Douglas LePan

The six poems in "A First Cluster of Love Poems" were first published in book form in *Something Still to Find*. The thirty-four poems in "A Last Cluster of Love Poems" are appearing here for the first time.

Canadian Cataloguing in Publication Data
LePan, Douglas, 1914-
   Far voyages

Poems.
ISBN 0-7710-5266-9

I. Title.

PS8523.E67F37 1989   C811'.54   C89-094748-1
PR9199.3.L45F37 1989

The publisher makes grateful acknowledgment to the Ontario Arts Council for its financial assistance.

Set in Kennerly by The Typeworks, Vancouver
Printed and bound in Canada

McClelland & Stewart Inc.
The Canadian Publishers
481 University Avenue
Toronto, Ontario M5G 2E9

In Memory

of

Patrick Fabbri

1948   1985

*

Bordeaux   *Montreal*

CONTENTS

Greetings

If I were coming to greet you out of antiquity
I would have in my hand a pomegranate for you, or a cockerel,
or a red-figured wine-cup with your name on it.
But since I am as I am, and live in Toronto,
I hope you'll settle for these clusters of love poems.

PRELUDE

A First Cluster of Love Poems

Song

I was whipped, I was whipped
      my brains were flayed
I was running like mad
      as the searchlights played
till I came to myself in the dark of your arms
      ah dancer, ah sweet dancer.

I was smashed, I was smashed
      my bones were sore
I was ready to fall
      I could stand no more
till I recovered my heart in the mesh of your mouth
      ah dancer, ah sweet dancer.

I was bushed, I was bushed
      I was dying alone
my blood had thickened
      I was turned to stone
till I felt on my flesh the print of your limbs
      ah dancer, ah sweet dancer.

I was crazed, I was crazed
      as I looked out on the street
at the switch-blade faces
      the trampling feet
I was poised on the edge when you swung me around
      ah dancer, ah sweet dancer.

Now the sweet dance of bodies
      given and taken
wide wash of nakedness

as we awaken
light lustrously, silkily, rippling between us
ah dancer, ah sweet dancer.

Lustrous and smooth
    your lover's art
but strong as chain-mail
    when we part
you, love, the armourer of my heart
    ah dancer, ah sweet dancer.

Leaves and Lyrics

Leaves protect me, lyrics shade me
from the angry god who made me.
Birds skim down with songs to save me,
sing me back the strength god gave me.

Nature joins both power and loving,
strong sap's beating, leaves' soft moving,
fold me in your green caressing
twine your veins and mine in blessing.

You are nature's child and minion,
strong your arm as eagle's pinion,
tender leaves your membranes beating,
our flushed veins two natures meeting.

I am yours for your green sheathing,
strong because of your sweet breathing,
new restored by your achieving;
a dark flower opens past believing.

Second Growth

A power-line marching through scrub,
that's what you've made me.

A transmission tower
crackling with messages, images.

A sunflower
aching sunward with seed.

A stricken tree
blossoming into flower and fruit.

Old limbs
new baptized into youth.

Passion of
a saviour streaming with blood.

Strength of
a saviour in a sheer white cloth.

Emblem

Wild orchid, veined with tenderness,
that reaches down to glacial rock
past moss and rotting ferns and pine-cones
and the droppings of porcupines, raccoons.

This your just signet, seal, and impress,
a moccasin plant on granite growing,
pink in the sun-shot shade of June,
frail trumpet, satin-smooth, and clear.

A flower, so fragile, soon will fade.
But while it lasts its fine-meshed membrane
both holds and hides a veined perfection,
a slipper that a prince might search for.

This emblem of the sensitive
and strong, triumphant short-lived song –
for you this emblem will not fade
but blazoning be and heraldry.

Aubade

Your name on my lips. Every night
as my eyes close. And the sweetness
of your body, as though you were with me.

Your name on my lips. Every morning,
waking, that one word on my lips.
I remember everything, everything.

But this morning there was nothing.
Then before I could think how strange it was
I was murmuring other words,

"Deeper than death or the dark,"
as though your mouth were on mine.
I love you that deeply, that deeply.

September Sunlight

It might almost be spring
the weather is so fine and lyric and sensual
with not a hint anywhere of decay or of dying,
bright, rather, with new faces setting off to classes
and rich with light cascading through green oak-leaves.

The air surrounds me like silk
as it twirls and untwirls (I might be a maypole)
in long gala streamers that attach me to you.
I turn in your direction, where you live now,
and feel on my face the faint glow of a sun-king.

I feel myself in the presence –
with the pride, at a distance, of a chosen favourite
who has yet to be fully acknowledged but whose face
has been brushed by the gold of secret election
like the gold of a moth's wing or of delicate sunburn.

Beyond the presence and palace
the markets are piled high with blue grapes
and with peaches as downy as the cheeks of epheboi.
Abundance floats in the air like a watermark,
I feel love from my fingertips dripping like milk.

FAR VOYAGES

A Last Cluster of Love Poems

Trial Brushstrokes

It's hard to capture you.
Glances that pierce but then melt into common day;
passages elusive as the sift of light through leaves;
an arpeggio of moods that are yet held in a classic calm;
an affectionate stippling on a ground of great constancy.
(But that brushwork isn't delicate enough.)

Let me try again, more indirectly.
In the spring, in a fold of the Laurentian granite,
where clumps of green moss grow as in the palm of a man's hand,
wild iris break into bloom, splitting open their green sheaths,
and triumph as if among a retinue of sword-bearers –
a strange coronation to spring from such rigour of rock.

Those falls and standards,
those tissues as delicate as silk around a sword-blade,
quiver with a more sensitive apprehension of what you are.
From something natural the flowering of something royal;
an ascesis of sensuality turning in the wind immaculately;
the glitter of a sword-edge that's never far from laughter.

That still isn't deft enough.
But it will have to serve as a first tentative shadowing
of what stays imaged, shimmering, in my heart of hearts –
a dark loyalty that's festal there in glints and glances;
a gallantry that waits to show its flags and colours;
a musk of aromatic virtue in root, stalk, and flower.

An Aside

Come close and I'll whisper it.
I hope that these poems will be neither slovenly nor pompous,
but easy and loquitive, so that you can carry them with you
          as you go back and forth on the *métro*.
(If that were to get out, I could be pilloried for hubris.)

And there's one other thing about them you should know.
They may start almost anywhere –
with a northern river, or a Doctor of the Church, or a soldier
going into action, or even with a little prolusion about fantasy and
          fact.
Don't worry, they'll be coming back to you soon enough.

Montale, you may remember, could turn a poem about almost
          anything
into a love poem. So why shouldn't I?

A Northern River, with Figures

Logged over, and then burnt over. Till all that's left
are scrub pin-oaks and jackpine over bare rock,
a scruffy landscape to serve as the high surround
for this river running down from Six Mile Lake.

But it brings with it sand and clay, sluiced down
by the spring run-offs, to make sandbars at its mouth
and to deposit a deep bed for the thread of the stream
and deep fertile banks for the summer vegetation.

That comes as the high season of metamorphosis.
Now it glides through a sweet cocoon of leaves,
past alders, and poplars, and towering birches –
a green palisade that quite blanks out the granite.

And the banks now are rich with Joe Pye weed,
great stands of it in abundance yard after yard,
their heliotrope flowers and tall purple stalks,
stiff, bending only a very little in the breeze,

but yet voluptuous, luxuriant, triumphant,
as though the whole scene had been transposed
to a different latitude and the kingfishers' clacking
to herald the canoe were now tropical, amazonian.

(Who Joe Pye was, seems to have been forgotten.
Some medicine man, I suppose, who was the first
perhaps to decoct from this imperial purple
an elixir of medicinal balms and balsams.)

The scene-shift could hardly be more fictive.
But it's not something longed for, imagined, not even
something achieved, but something simply bestowed,
a gift from the spring freshets and the strengthening
    sun.

And that was the way that you entered my life,
gratuitously, not as something I richly deserved
for hard work, or suffering, or labours accomplished.
You came very quietly to blot out the granite.

I don't like to recall all the years that my life
ran through bare rock. Perhaps some might say
I made it that way myself, raised up its ridges
and whalesbacks, made it even that way for others.

Perhaps. Yet I doubt it. I prefer to arraign
the wars, and rumours of wars, and wars' aftermath,
leaving deep scars and parasites. That was what
ruined "a fine gentleman," almost ruined a poet.

It was you who gave me back summer, and ease,
and refreshment. A blithe featheriness of leaves turning
in the wind. A playfulness of green foliage hiding
grey rock. A lithe natural heroism of rippling

strength as if to fulfill a tree-spirit's dream.
A sweet elixir from such savage flowers decocted
as would medicine me back to wholeness, coaxing
my foiled valiancy to turn once more to the sun.

A Map with New Provinces

Your sides sloping away beneath my hands
   are another world with provinces of delight
      sweet with the suave washes of a coloured map,
         with pale salmon pinks or strawberry reds,
            under the light gold of your body-hair.

Strangers perhaps might people these new provinces
   with all manner of exotic deliciousness,
      with pomegranates or nectarines or persimmons;
         hang them with cressets; or see there
            the dire panthers that roam in Cilicia.

Yes, they are other. But to me they're as familiar
   as warm pastures in old Ontario or Quebec,
      where wild strawberries are lurking in early July;
         or shanties in the sugar-bush for the sugaring-off;
            or farm-kitchens with taffy astir on the stove.

Fields where we both have been happy. It's that magic
   that invests them with triumph, that and the gleam
      from your swimmer's limbs in a bright surf of sun,
         that makes so perpetually lustrous these provinces,
            as though death's dark *imperium* had been dazzled away.

Flames, at the Beginning

I am burning your letter, as you asked me to.
In the light through the window it flames up like a great
      gold chrysanthemum.
Our love will flourish like that, extravagant and secret.

A Sheer Coincidence

"It is delicate and silky, yet full-bodied,
and has a rich bouquet, with hints of apricot and raspberry."
No, that isn't about you or anything of yours, if you're wondering.
But it made me laugh out loud the moment I read it
(in a flyer about French wines) the words would fit you so exactly,
your full-bodied strength, your touch so delicate and silky,
the fresh bouquet of your naked honour and honesty.

As an exercise in the playfulness that, as I say,
you're giving back to me, I swirl the words lightly round
and round on my tongue; and the more I taste them, the more
apposite they seem. Even the following remark that "its luscious
        depth
owes much to the granite-based soil" is right on target, too,
since I have reason to know how much of your sun-ripened
        strength
has matured over a footing of Laurentian rock.

Chrysostom

Golden mouth. The name of the honey-tongued
saint who was driven out into exile.

Golden mouth. Said of a French poet
of the high Middle Ages as he lay sleeping.

Golden mouth to golden mouth. Our mouths
as they searched out each other.

By putting your lips to mine,
you have brought me back from the drowse of exile,

and opened my lips, the lips of a poet,
to sing – and to show forth your praise.

A Stream of Images

It was someone speaking of your picture.
". . . like a bodhisattva who sits impassive
on the flowering lotus, with lids half-closed,
who now could enter into nirvana
but absents himself instead to stay
on earth with suffering humankind."
And with that image I am filled with peace
and calm, as deep as I breathed one evening
at a guest-house in Ceylon, watching
a young man in a sarong of shadowy
madras cross through the lamplit dark
to pray and sacrifice beneath a bo-tree.

Images of gilt, of gold, of watery bronze

Or an image of the charioteer at Delphi,
his tunic falling in bronze fabric-folds
of lyrical severity, his hair bound back
by the victor's fillet, the reins still dangling,
his eyes fixed in serenity, unsurprised,
held in an almost other-worldly calm.
And that gaze calls up the sacred way,
the sacred cleft, the sacred spring,
and above the temenos the eagles circling,
screaming – a dark cascade of rock and pine
that, some say, was long held to be divine
before Apollo had his temple there.

Images of athletes, gods, and heroes

An image of the risen Christ, triumphant,
who, having harrowed Hell, now stands
with one foot resting on the empty tomb

(as Piero frescoed Him at Borgo San
Sepolcro), looking into the eye of the sun
and into the equal eye of God the Father,
of the earth earthy, of heaven heavenly,
still wearing the five wounds like scarlet seals,
with the long dark locks of the *homo silvaticus*,
the man from the woods, the sylvan man,
that Green Man who always makes me think
of runners through our own green wilderness.

       Images of wounds, of wounds transcended

A pinetree springing from a rock-face,
rooted in the fissures there, but towering
skyward above the swiftly flowing river
(as our love is held fast in flesh and blood
but reaches up towards heaven) high as
a spire, close to the clouds that mirror
the cumulus of the river's falls and chutes
and the sailing gulls that must have made
Champlain think that he was coming to a sea.
And so he was, to a broad sweetwater sea —
where a comet's tail of *coureurs de bois*
would follow in his wake beneath the pinetree.

       Images emerging from dense wilderness

It's because of you these images return,
images of clay, or watery bronze, of gold,
images of athletes, gods, and heroes,
images of wounds, of wounds transcended,
images emerging from green wilderness
but then opening like the flowering lotus,

like water-lilies at the margins of our lakes,
into pure radiance as at the world's
first morning, fresh, vivid, undismayed,
instinct with love and vision that make
them flow, yet hold them in a flowing
timeless river. Because of you this stream of

Images returning
Images of the hero and the river

Bright Shining Things

All bright shining things are yours today,
or else become you in the dazzle of the light spring breeze
and the sunlight on the water. As I walked down the road, the
      birds came close.
Circling a few feet above me, flamed the brand of a red-winged
      blackbird,
flashing its blazons, scarlet and gold, in the morning sun,
chattering and chuckling – out of anger or friendly boldness? Hard
      to say.
But I went on crowned by that military aureole, proud and
      exulting.
Though I wasn't thinking of you, you entered my eye, you entered
      my bloodstream.
The bird, and the morning sunlight, and I – all were yours, were
      you.

Then I came to a field with the sun golden in the grass
where a friendly flicker waited for me on a fence-post, waited
until I could see the scarlet patch at the top of its broad brown
      back
and then, as it flew on to a further fence-post – rising and dipping
      and rising –
from the underside of its wings shook out its golden shining.
Marvellous! and a marvel in which you were implicit,
whether because the bird's gold feathers were chevroned across
      your ribs,
or because the light in your eye, the spring in your step, the russet
      in your hair,
infected my seeing, making all Nature seem more scintillant, more
      alive,

I couldn't tell. But the two brightnesses colliding there lived as
      one,
rippling, glittering, quivering, breathing,
a single wave in sunlight that was still combing, cresting, breaking,
      falling.

Now the wind freshens, and the sparkle on the water.
Gone are the mare's-tails low on the horizon. The sky is flawless.
A deep pulse overhead quivers throughout the heavens like a
      watermark.
Blasphemy or not, the naked flawless sky is quivering with your
      image.
I watch the sunlight break over the waves, and the waves break
      over the shoals,
and know love flowing everlastingly, but everlastingly the same.

Perceptions of Contrast

White birches glimmering among dark green pines:
thoughts of you lighting up the dark snarls and tangles
        of my brain,
nerve-ends to branching nerve-ends quivering in contrast:
white birches, dark green pines.

Literally

"You're all the world to me."
Yes, I mean it. The United Nations and its 14 specialized agencies
    (count them!);
and General Dynamics and the whole "military-industrial
    complex";
and, coming nearer home, Power Corporation and all its
    subsidiaries
(including Consolidated-Bathurst and *La Presse* and Great-West
    Life Assurance);
and the empires of the Bronfmans and the Reichmanns and the
    Thomsons;
and all the fluttery coteries of the economic nationalists.
I wouldn't trade you for the lot of them, or for any one of them,
or for the United States Sixth Fleet, or "the German economic
    miracle,"
or the Japanese ditto, or the Toronto Stock Exchange, or the
    Montreal Stock Exchange.

I know what I'm talking about, and I tell you
none of them are worth the powder to blow them to hell compared
    with
what you are to me − and that's all the world. I mean it.

Virtuoso

So many roles...

a great virtuoso, diver or flute-player,
apt for light airs and gallantry;

but with shoulders
strong enough for the storms
when the masts are goring and tossing the clouds,
hands strong enough
for the knotted salted cordage
when the hull is groaning in agony from keel to forepeak,
the seas battering it and the winds,
the whole ship groaning in triumph like a taut hawser breaking.

So many roles and played so dextrously,
in and out from one to another, hardly ever missing a beat,
sure of each role's inflection, your pitch is so true –
Hamlet, Horatio; Marsyas, Apollo; minion, athlete, prince.
The secret is virtuosity – yes, but great constancy too.

According to La Rochefoucauld

Constancy in love is of two kinds

                      wrote terse La Rochefoucauld.
One is like an inexhaustible spring and comes from constantly
      finding
new things to love in the one you love. The other comes from
making it a point of honour to be constant. (And you might want
to remember that he was a soldier before turning aphorist.)

So the parts are evenly divided between us, dear comrade-in-arms.
But my part is far easier than yours. I'm constantly finding
in you new things to love, new drolleries, new endurances.
While you?

             Free as you are, and as I want you to be,
I'm afraid there must be many times when constancy for you
comes down to a point of honour.

Wolves and Knives

When you're away, the wind longs for you
and I long for you.
I walk the dark streets, eating
my heart out with longing
till it gnaws like a wolf at my breast.

Our freshwater wind has turned into
a wolf from the sea
that lusts after you here and there,
and rubs salt in the wound
like a sea wind hankering for sailors.

Here is a city of wolves and knives –
so it seems when you're gone.
The knives of resentment are unsheathed
and hiss in my hand.
Wolves with their red tongues go prowling.

It was I who wanted you to be free,
who loosed you in love
to come and go whenever you pleased.
So why should I resent
the freedom I so wantonly gave you?

I do, though. And bitterness blinds me.
The leaves drop from the trees.
The dark streets are slippery with wet
leaves and the shine of tears.
Long since the pale moon dropped from the sky.

I confess to my shame that I'm jealous
of those that you're with now,
even of the chandeliers
that light up your auburn hair
and the glint of your sweet other tongue.

That's how lost I am in your absence.
But when you return!...
you come back like a prince returning
with the pulse blue in your veins
and bright guineas in all of your pockets.

There's gold that day floats in the air,
the gold from your hands
and your lips, and your sun-pollened limbs,
that make it all up to me;
there's gold, too, from my heart's wild hosannas.

Walking a Tightrope

The delicate wavering line between fantasy and fact,
a line that has to be redrawn almost every time
that the house-lights go down and the scene is made
to glow from within the phosphor of kindled passion.

What is needed as kindling is fantasizing that may have
been smouldering for days, and may persist till the final act,
or perhaps well beyond. The trick is to let it ignite
and illumine, without ever letting it burn the house down.

It's as though the boundary between two sovereign states
had to be redrawn at every encounter. Or, better still, as though
the line between settlement and wilderness were endlessly shifting,
with now the palefaces, and now the redskins, advancing.

It's a little the same, but not quite, as the strict dramatic
tension between illusion and reality, between Theseus' world
and Oberon's and Titania's, between the world of the lawgiver
and their wildwood realm of illusion and metamorphosis,

where what you imagine, what you desire, can happen,
does happen, but also where a clumsy artisan can be tricked
into absurdity, as he rehearses his interlude – a performance
of one mimesis in the arms of another, mirror echoing mirror.

To come nearer home, I think of Blondin crossing the Falls,
his tightrope swaying in the wind, a long pole steadying him;
and of his audience (who now are part of the performance);
young gentlemen of delicate sensibility in wide-awake hats

(I wonder what their fantasies are?); and the young ladies with
        them
in Paisley shawls; and then behind them a scuffle of rubes
and suckers, with hucksters of cheap souvenirs and candy-floss
to add a rank demotic flavour to the thin mist from the Falls;

all watching Blondin, with his powerful thighs, as he glides
out along the rope as if he were a dancer in ballet slippers
and then runs to do a dancer's leap over the Gorge, till one
viewer after another asks in astonishment, "What is real?"

Well, what is? What is real in this shadowy engagement,
not only between two agonists, but between their fantasies
and their physical entanglement, where the inner stage is a bed
now fresh as green balsam tips, now soaking in sweat?

You are, for one thing. What gives coherence to the action
is you at its centre, deft, skilful, affectionate, a creature
of fantasies (like me!), but able to make our different fantasies
so clasp and intertwine that they bind us closer together.

Gross as they may be, or of gossamer fineness, the stuff
of our dreams, you're never afraid of them. You play to them
like a snake-charmer, handling them proudly in their speckled
sinuous glory as though they too were sent by a god.

You know all about the ballets and masques at court,
_ masques interspersed with antimasques, with ballets of courtiers
followed by ballets of beasts, at the pleasure of princes.
But you never forget that what matters most is the moment

when the mist of our fantasies (which are easier to manage
here where the actors are their own directors, and where roles
can be tossed back and forth freely) is suddenly burned off
in the great lion glare of naked carnality, and when

your eyes (like mine!) are drilled right down to the soul,
the sovereign self is surrendered, and each offers the other
not only strength, secrecy, repose, but whatever it knows
of godhead, that godhead that burns in your thighs like a bush.

Two Cities

Now that we've decided to turn this into a tale of two cities
and commute back and forth between Toronto and Montreal
it occurs to me that we've made a typically Canadian compromise.
Toronto? Montreal?
                              We'll divide our favours between them.
One month will see us walking along Sherbrooke Street
and the next month along Bloor Street, with equal urbanity.
In that way, no one will have any cause for complaint,
neither the good burghers of Toronto, nor their counterparts
in Montreal. The two hockey teams may be at each other's throats,
and the two stock exchanges. Even the two symphonies and the
         two
ballet-companies have sometimes been not all that friendly.
But, given your sweetness of temper, it would be a pity, I think,
to let you become another source of contention.
And I'm quite content that your lustre be shared between
my native city – with its lakefront and wide viaducts and
         ravines –
and the city of your parents' adoption, the proud city of the
         mountain
and the river, the majestically flowing "River of Canada."

So where does that leave the score between the two cities?
Add in. Add out. And so it could go on and on . . .
As for us, let's leave the game undecided – at deuce.

Winter Day, Montreal

Framed by the parlour-car window, I look out at the city
I'm leaving as though it were adrift in a frozen calm.

It's so windless the vapours from stacks and chimneys spire
straight up into a powder-blue heaven that the sun

is frosting with light to heighten the red-tufted tuques
of boys on their way to school – or to hockey practice –

and the dark brown blush of fur-coats struggling up
Beaver Hall Hill (where the Nor' Westers schemed and caroused).

The dominant colour is blue, though, the light blue of the sky,
and the dark blue, almost black, of ice on the canal and the river,

so that at moments the buildings are ice-floes afloat
on the shimmering surface of a tranced ultramarine sea.

But – what confusion of seasons is this? – I'm still
tasting, still have the taste in my mouth of *fraises des bois,*

of the sweetness lurking under leaves in the last days of spring
or the first days of summer, a sweetness brought out by heat;

I still taste the honeysuckle savour of our last conversation,
of a rosy expectancy, of a strong quivering anticipation,

that, consummated, still lives on the palate. A strong delirium
of tissues opening, unfolding, like petals, like brief mortal petals.

Wild orchids, opening, unfolding, in the deep shade of sun
over rock. A deep memory of rosy delicate veinings.

This morning, as I leave you and your city to go back to my own,
I feel as though it's the spring I've been sleeping with,

and I ask myself why, even in Canada, the logic of winter
should be thought so superior to the logic of summer – or spring?

A Diesel Whistling on a May Morning

Some days are so beautiful they could break your heart.

It was that way as I was leaving Toronto this morning,
the limestone distillery on my left (where they still make
      "Canadian Club"),
and on my right the long run out along the lakefront,
the streams full and gushing, some fields golden with dandelions
and others golden with buttercups, the marshes stippled with
      marsh marigolds;
and the red-winged blackbirds back, flashing and lighting and
      tilting
on last year's cat's-tails (their tops now ragged and woolly
like wool socks pulled inside out); a day of bright sunshine
and calm mild airs above a delicately disciplined landscape,
a day of light clouds melting into each other like lovers,
a day so beautiful you might have dreamed it all up for me.

All of it marvellous
as desire licked up the miles, desire licked up the tracks.

The diesel blowing its whistle most of the way
(to tell you I'm coming?) tally ho! tally ho! tally ho!
It made me think of huntsmen or of Dickensian coaching-scenes,
the coachman whipping on the horses, and the post-boy blowing
      his horn
almost incessantly as they swept past one bend after another,
lickety-split, lickety-split, until we sailed into a whole
plantation of trilliums, fresh galaxies of them
on both sides of the tracks, millions of them, trillions of them,
the birth of new galaxies at the edge of the green woodlots
bordering the railway line, called into brief being (like

ephemeral Potemkin villages to grace our whirlwind triumphant
progress), called into being by the diesel's whistle – or by
a post-boy's long slim coaching-horn?

Was there a postillion, perhaps, as well?
I couldn't tell. I don't think so. But there might have been.

Let's add a postillion, then – in a tunic of red and gold
and a black velvet jockey-cap (dating back to the days of
          Charles II);
a postillion able to crush the morning's diffused vivacity
into a single terse muscular torso, compressing its magic,
and to whip the diesel's crude oily energy and velocity
into the more supple rhythms of a centaur's bare haunches;
a postillion with the power to translate the trilliums' three
white floppy petals and three green equally floppy leaves
– as we crossed the Ottawa River at Ste. Anne de Bellevue –
into something immediately more erect and spruce and heraldic,
into white fleur-de-lis, no less, on a sky-blue ground.
And it goes without saying, of course, that a postillion like that
would know that, however many or sharp the bends,
however raucous the rasp of the couplings, by subtle
tricks of perspective the diesel's whistling trajectory
and the tracks converging were all today aimed straight at you.

Forgive me if I seem a little out of breath on arrival.
It's partly desire, of course. But not only that. I think
I'm a little over-excited from the beauty of the day, and the
diesel whistling, and perhaps from some over-indulgence in
          equestrian imagery.

Skyblue Spaces

Strange, how you snare the sun like a bird-catcher!
Blue sky in your rib-cage. Blue sky between your temples
bathing your mind in a strong and supple clearness
so that it shares in a wise light both human and divine.
Translucencies of sun all through you. Who have been
his creature for so many hours on so many beaches, you bring
the captor captive, the tyrant tamed, your sunburned body
starred with all the signs in all twelve houses that his course
runs through – the Lamb, Bull, Lion, Water-carrier and the rest...
That bright ecliptic runs clear through you.

You wince a little. Do you find those claims excessive?
the style too hyperbolic? the mood a trifle too assertive?
Then try to remember the problem that I'm wrestling with:
the theme that I was given and have become inured to
was loss; perfection vanishing; wounds; the scoring on frail
flesh of peacock greens and blues; those dreams dissolving,
fading, dissolving into the light of common day –
and all that reaching far far back, into a region
far older than the peacock crest on the family ring I wear.
But now from a clear sky again the oracle has spoken.
The theme has changed. To happiness achieved; strength; health;
fable become fact; the unbelievable become the simple truth;
dreams made incarnate; being wounded transformed to
being healed. In the land I'm called to, all the mutations
now are favourable, steel becomes silk and yet remains
strong. Common day persists. But those peacock greens and blues
persist as well. Persist into the heart of light. Persist
into the heart of common day, unfading.

And I am set musing on white columns above a wine-dark sea.
(Far voyages! Out from the centre of my surrendered self.)
And on a style, still barely glimpsed, where words and meaning
would fit like a glove – no, closer than that, like light –
sound fitting sense like light across the back of your hand
(felicities of style to match the happiness you've brought me);
on a poetry of such enraptured order, such sure inflections,
turning now this way and now that, now to fable now to fact,
now to dreaming and now to dawn, now to iridescence
and now to common day, each shining through its opposite,
a poetry fit to build a wide free-floating crystalline
geodesy, of rainbow lightness but of steely strength
where every facet every plane would mirror every other...

But enough for now of those far fancies.
My gaze comes home to where you're lying on the beach,
to your simple presence (snaring the sun with your honeyed limbs),
to your muscles rippling over your ribs,
and to the pale turquoise waves as they come rippling up over the
        sand.

In a Summer Night

A moth's wing idly crushed between my fingers.
And with that the whole room lights up in sudden amorous glory.
It must be remembering how earlier in the day it glowed like a
      sunflower
with the rich light quickening on your pollened forearm.

Passacaglia

I love it when you tell me you love me. But there's no need.
I can tell that from the way you move when we're alone.
But what's harder is trying to figure out *why* you love me,
someone so weatherbeaten, so morose, so footsore and heartsore
from the journey, living only from day to day, accustomed
to loss and disappointment, hardly expecting anything else,
with hardly anything more than a soldier's low horizons.
But even now that you've utterly changed the prospect,
and (with a little help from me) broken down my dour carapace
and mollified the proud flesh round my wounds, there's still
plenty of scar-tissue left. So...why? But the very question
may well be rather ridiculous, a hangover from a different
life and a different habit of discourse, before the old terms
and categories were radically altered. As well ask perhaps,
Why are the upper staves of the passacaglia in love
with the seemingly sullen bass? Or, why is the aria
in love with the accompaniment? The free-floating tenor
or coloratura aria, that has a wealth of playful
or spirited *fioriture* and brilliant cadenzas; the accompaniment
that simply seems to rock back and forth, back and forth,
and has little more to say for itself than that. Yet together
they make something out of this world, with its own pulse
and breathing, different from ours, yet leading us on,
showing us the way into a delectable transient clearing,
the skies a halcyon azure, but with traces of passionate scarlet.
Now I'm learning to stop asking questions and simply
to listen to the music. And it's full of surprises. Sometimes
it's rowdy with kettledrums, sometimes placid as a sunlit lake,
sometimes as deftly inconsequent as a long poem by Frank
O'Hara. But whatever it is, you make it all *cantabile*.
I waken to ethereal music, to bird-song as though

flutes were conversing with oboes, or to murmurings,
raptures, that seem even more heavenly, more profound.
I look up surprised, to see that there's a helicopter overhead,
trailing a long sign that reads lazily, "No more questions, please."

Voices in a Cantata

As if trumpets cried round your limbs
scarlet, fortissimo, in a passionate military fanfare.

But then the air round them becomes gentle as oboes,
as mild and caressing as the deep blue sobs of oboes d'amore.
And then sometimes there's a brisk hornpipe in your eyes,
acknowledging pleasure, glittering like sunlight on a lake.

What gnosis is brought by these various voices?
when your limbs with music intertwining, suggest
interlacings of so many possible kinds – of lovers interlaced,
or the interlacing of reconciled body and soul, or the union
of sensuousness with muscularity, as they cohere, so closely cohere,
in all of the music that I most admire?

That gnosis must remain a mystery.
But let others take note,
                    these mysteries of ours have their own cantatas.

Broken Music

Finding you
was like finding a diamond in the grass,

the grass of nature sparkling
through a mist of prisms;

or like finding a lyric fragment
in sands of the desert,

a lost love lyric
on a sheet of torn papyrus;

or like finding a peacock's feather
after a night of anguish,

lying there as a reminder
of animal pride and splendour.

And those comparisons for finding you
could go on and on...

But for losing you?...
there's no comparison for that, not one.

Falcons Fly Heavenward

Going into action, a soldier may take out his life and set it to one
side (as you might take off a watch and lay it on a table) in
the hope of picking it up again, if all goes well, when the
battle is over;

but now it's a forfeit, a forfeit paid in advance, a forfeit paid to
ensure that in the hazards of action he won't be
encumbered by calculation, by any need to be counting the
cost.

Or a falconer will loose a falcon from his wrist and let it fly
heavenward, towering and soaring, as if it were his honour
paid to the majesty of the sun, paid in the coin of a faithful
liegeman.

So we shed one after another aspects of our selfhood, knowing
they are safe in each other's keeping, knowing that
afterwards we can pick them all up again, the regalia of an
immaculate restoration.

Falcons fly heavenward, shielding us with their golden shining.

Bravado of Spring

Leaves falling, snowflakes falling, tears falling –
that sounds the whole gamut, it seems,
of the love of quite a few I could mention,
theirs is so delicate, so refined.

But ours?
            It has the weight and breathing of bulls.
It has the vascular glory of spring and of sap writhing from the
      earth.
It bursts like a grenade in a drawing-room, bringing down the bric-
      à-brac.
It explodes with all the fury of blossoming chestnut or flowering
      crab.
It brays of blood like a cut pomegranate or a scarlet tunic.

And who ever heard of a trooper caring for leaves falling, or
      snowflakes, or tears?
There'll be time enough for that when we're both in our graves.

Fête de Nuit

A fistful of stars spurts over the Seine like a tiger-lily.
That was a night of festival, years ago.

And now. . .a night like a festival on an arm of the sea.
A blue night, blue and watery and moony. Fountains and
      fireworks,
though most of the walks through the fairgrounds are dusky, almost
      dark.
And glimpsed only dimly, dreamily, a large tricolour, unfurling
      lazily,
now veined a deep-sea-blue and rippled by the night-wind passing,
now hard and red and gleaming, now pale in the fleecy moonlight.
And a carousel with golden dolphins, and a golden ring. And a
      fun-fair
with a lucky dip, and a great gong to be made cry out if you have
      the strength,
cry out in the moment when the fireworks drop from the branching
      peak
of their great arc. And all around and always the delicate lapping
of waves like lips in all the inlets.

You are all that. And more. A hero from legend playing with a
      clutch
of serpents. A summer shower of meteors. Galactic wonder.
A new universe unfolding. Bewilderment of nebulae, of star-shine.
Annunciation arrowing. The blue felicity of light.

Afterwards

Dark dreams, dark stars, the whole sky falling,
these in your closed eyes cluster.

Nights of Hercules! But now the lull and swell after storm,
a deep tideless sea that moves beyond furious pillars.

Now you lie utterly becalmed and firm and still,
firm as a breathing bronze in the water sleeping,

but all unarmed and tender – with only me to guard you –
exhaling still the salt-spray sweetness of our loving.

As we drift towards sleep together, we touch or talk or doze,
two astronauts floating down as the world resumes

in heavier and heavier atmospheres of air and ocean,
yet free from all taint and wash of worry, absolved

and purified as the sweet of the night flows in,
bathing our thighs, our eyes in dark gratitudes of starlight.

The ceiling of the room now melts into the sky,
the surface of our world tonight floats fathoms high.

Your Image among Islands

A winter afternoon of overcast and depression...
a seagull floats through the overcast between green islands,
between grey-green islands white wings floating like petals,
petals of flowering dogwood, far south, in early spring.

A Skein of Contraries

As shameless as a scarlet coat,
as shameful as torn tousled sheets,

our love is stitched of contraries
like colours in a country quilt.

A winter-palace to keep us warm
a summer-palace of leafy light.

An agony of cries and fission,
an ecstasy of perfect fusion.

Tart to the tastebuds as another tongue,
but soft, and yielding.

Salty as seaweed, but sweet, too,
sweet as the shore is to survivors.

Blaze to light up a darkened room
then fading to the light of planets

that pencil in a temenos
where every lust is holy, holy,

where proudly in the dusk
we strip away our plumes of pride,

lie down anonymous to find ourselves
and rise more surely what we are,

from durance pluck deliverance,
are locked in freedom, die to live,

drink from a clear spring laced with juniper,
learn from a serpent rustling through the fern.

Lords and Commons

Will you tease me if I say you have natural *noblesse*? –
an aura that moves with you everywhere you move,
singling out your presence with rare delicate decision
and adding to your grace a trace of the blood royal,

so that your occasions from one day to the next
seem often to be floating against dextrously woven
unicorns in meadows fleur-de-lis'd with flowers,
where you tread lightly, never putting a foot wrong,

greeting whomever you meet, whether lords or commons,
with the same courtesy – tinged with innocent mischief –
as though you were a wanderer from a more chivalrous age,
but having given your *parole* you would someday return.

You may smile, but it's true. In your simplest acts
there lurks a sword-edge of battlements and scaling-ladders,
a rustling of subtle brocades in audience-chambers,
a chivalric virtue that flows straight from your heart.

It flowers from the tissues of those valves and chambers
as surely as it did through the blue veins and arteries
of that Lion Hearted king with the lean leopard device
who could make songs – and love – as well as storm castles,

whose attributes in war and peace, so the chroniclers
say, were a rare courage and liberality and constancy;
and those gifts are yours, too – whether in the traffic
of your daytime occasions or in the dark play of *jouissance*.

The chronicler and romancers, I know, may make more
of the chivalric virtues than the brute facts will allow.
And there can be futility in castle after castle besieged,
in castles lost, and then won, and then lost again.

But to make something out of a land of unmeaning,
is there more to be hoped for than that? And isn't that
what we've managed together? From the grasp of unmeaning
to have wrestled and wrung a trust, an indenture

that can seem thin as paper, yet has life of its own,
is a bond, where the two halves, the two stanzas, fit perfectly,
where the song sung from inside the castle answers
to the one sung by the *jongleur* from under the wall.

Hours plucked from the tree of time, to be made
immortal! Hours flushed with your auburn magic!
Hours where we've had the courage to swan out
beyond reason and discourse in our love for each other!

Lords, dukes, and princes all have their suzerain
rights and distinctions. But they, like the commons,
are yet subject to one ultimate human supremacy,
to the ultimate human need to love and be loved.

Chain-mail can chafe. And at the end of the day
even the Lion Hearted, when he'd stripped off his armour,
would lie down as proudly and simply as we do
in the strong naked enchantment of a sworn lover's arms.

Dread

Down into dread together.

Now as you battle with insurgent cells, that grim
guerrilla war (slashed sometimes by surgeon's steel
and screams as you waken from Demerol) is imaged in me.
In labyrinthine disorders and vertigo, a swirling abyss,
in arterial spasms and tightenings, the blood racing and pounding.

And even when your attacks are in remission, even then
(strange that you should now be the soldier, and I the *embusqué*!)
in spite of your courage and endurance, I'm riddled with fear,
fear of your being lost to me, fear of your being badly hurt,
though you stand it like a veteran, the long nausea of combat.

It's a strange kind of sundance, a harsh leathery sundance,
as the subtleties of referred pain bind us together, the thongs
looped under my chest, the pain round my heart, circling
your pain, as if hoping to restore a clouded brightness,
as if to restore a young sun-king to his youthful vigour.

Apart, yet we've never been drawn so close together.
Down into dread, now we go down into dread together.

Dead of Night

Don't leave me, don't leave me,
that's what I say over and over.
And never more so than after
a dream that I had last night
where a torso half-muffled by the sea,
cloud muffling his face,
was being washed to and fro
in waves of ungilded *grisaille*
while a voice from a distance
was saying, "He is leaving us . . ."
And I awoke trembling and terrified,
trying to hold back hysteria, trying
to be half as stoical as you are,
but in truth being beside myself
with animal fury and animal anguish.
The wolves come out of the darkness,
I am become their poor creature.
If you were to leave me, how could
I ever find the strength to go on?
Or even the strength for that last act
of love – and grief and homage –
to distance your image and free it in air?

Serenissima

How far we've voyaged!

Into the rank bosom of the Serenissima
                            and out to the limits of savagery.

To the blowsy glory of the city sinking into the sea,
of all sensualities the ripest, richest in the world,
the brass of Gabrieli still vibrating, the ripe rich palette
of Titian and Veronese still pulsing, throbbing, as colour
drains in and out of the Piazza like sift in an hourglass,
and all enriched by the stench of piles and timbers rotting,
the squandered opulence of ten centuries on the polluted waves
(to say nothing of gas from the refineries being flared off
the day we came, or of the *bacino* gorged with an aircraft-
carrier of the United States Sixth Fleet and its supply ship
the day we left), with cunning goldsmiths and cunning glass-
      blowers
still offering choice refinements for all the pleasures of the senses.
Ah! Serenissima, continual cunning temptress.

Voyages . . . far voyages together . . .

Out to the limits of savagery. From Ile-à-la-Crosse,
where the river pitches down, untamed, to Hudson Bay,
where the voyageurs' canoes raced through the rapids, gravid
with furs, and they avid for the debauchery of Grand Portage,
the *gouvernail* standing in the stern to steer with his long
slim blade, the *avant* dextrous to choose between one channel
and another, and all of them, *bourgeois, milieux,* all,
half-crazed with the delirium of white water and their precious
freedom (paid for with risk and danger), freedom

from church and state and family, as they go hurtling through
the rapids. And there was danger enough the year we risked it,
high water, the river in spate, the portage landings flooded,
the danger of being swamped or of being broken in the eddies.

Far, far voyages...

The latitudes of love, those are by far the hardest to invoke.
But I remember, as I know you do too, the soft trade winds
blowing around the beaches of one of the Sugar Islands,
almost always blowing but always softly softly, awakening
the scent of limes but hardly ruffling the year-long blossoms
of the bougainvillaeas, rose-red or heliotrope or coral.
From where you're lying on the sand, the sea seems turquoise
first, then azure, deeper azure, and at the far horizon deep
deep indigo, a spawning sea both prodigal and equivocal,
the source and sanction of everything there is in nature,
pluming itself in all the colours of the sky's anathemas –
till night falls and we ride toward sleep in a deep sea of love,
the soft sea breeze and soft sea surf our only coverlet.

Far voyages...

And now down into dread, down into dread together,
a steep glissade that's drawing us down, down, down.
What is this landscape, colourless, giddily descending,
pot-holed with vertigo, and with sickening falls and chutes,
where I'm lurching dizzily from one door-post to another,
and, far away, you're battling with your lymph's insurgency
– so far apart! yet never drawn so close together –
battling your heart out, giving it all you have,

even to the marrow of your bones? And your heart's tumult
is mirrored in mine, in my heart's sombre echo-chambers,
my arteries in spasm, my heart-muscles stiffening, groaning.
Had we ever foreseen these marches, these desolate marches?
A sad sick landscape, a landscape almost of despair.

But sometimes early in the morning, at first light,
comes a moment of serenity and calm self-surrender.
I look out the hospital window to see places where we've been
together, though the world and the things of this world are
      vanishing,
all but eyes that I know
                  lips that I know
                              a face that I know.

The world, and the storms of this world, and the fleets of this
      world,
                          fade on the morning breeze
leaving only a low voice calling *gondola gondola*
                    and then even more softly gently
                    andiamo andiamo

and then from far far in the distance
                    caro mio dilectissimo.

Portrait, in a Frame of Distance

In a moment of calmness, of clearness,
you escape from the cunning nets that I weave for you,
gross sensual nets, fine-meshed nets of the spirit,
and shine out in your own immaculate selfhood,
that's fleshed so fair, yet is so sensitive, stoical.
(Even now, it's still hard to capture you.)

In the space that spreads lustrous around you
there's room for the olives of Lucca, the clusters of Bordeaux,
to ripen in continuing freshness. They still quicken the flow
of your beautiful Tuscan and the deft loquitive sweetness
you first learnt as a schoolboy in Paris. And from where else
comes your wit and your grave *sprezzatura*?

But there's more in your eyes than a grave
playful serenity. There's distance. And that draws its source,
I would guess, from more northerly skies, from ski-slopes where
you take the turns with such handsome assurance, and from
canoe-routes reaching back to the musk of the fur-trade –
and to white water and long savage portages.

When I try to think of you as you are
(and try to forget the print of your body on mine,
of your spirit on mine, which will be with me to the end)
what comes to me is a manner that's graceful, teasing, amusing;
a nature that's as profoundly affectionate as passionate;
and a strong deep courage clear as a whistle.

If I were a painter, I would place you
in a background of subtlest tempera, hung with persimmons,
and would allow the windless calm to be disturbed only by

a faint dust raised by carriage-wheels in the middle distance,
a gilt carriage travelling in style from God knows where,
with spruce outriders in liveries all of olive-green.

But your image in its freedom of air
calls more for a sculptor. Then it could be turned through space.
And through time. And out of time. Until in timelessness
it would shine out, unfading, the modelling of your face
now captured at last, as the planes of your cheeks and your temples
commune with the planes of eternity.